Apple Tree Farm

the highest point of the track

the old track

Bellamy's Changing World: The Roadside
was conceived, edited and designed by Frances Lincoln Limited
Apollo Works, 5 Charlton Kings Road, London NW5 2SB

First published in Great Britain by
Macdonald and Co. (Publishers) Ltd,
Greater London House,
Hampstead Road,
London NW1 7RX
A BPCC plc Company

British Library Cataloguing in Publication Data

Bellamy, David *1933* —
The roadside — (Bellamy's Changing World: 3)
1. Natural history — Juvenile literature
2. Roadside flora — Juvenile literature
3. Roadside fauna — Juvenile literature
I. Title   II. Dow, Jill   III. Series
574.9   QH48

ISBN 0-356-13568-3

Printed and bound in Italy

Design and Art Direction Debbie Mackinnon

Frances Lincoln Ltd. would like to thank
Pippa Rubinstein, Trish Burgess, Sarah Mitchell,
Kathy Henderson, Kathryn Cave, Stephen Pollock
and Jackie Westbrook for help with the series.

Bellamy's Changing World

The
Roadside

David Bellamy

with illustrations by Jill Dow

Macdonald

It's midsummer and just off the main road, two kinds of countryside meet at this gate. In the field a crop of wheat is nearly ripe. Soon the machinery will be brought in to harvest the grain and take it away to store. The track goes on to the right and is rarely used. It leads to Apple Tree Farm but the big company that farms the land today doesn't

use the buildings. The farmhouse is deserted and the partly overgrown track is a perfect home for all sorts of wildlife. Butterflies and other insects feed on the nectar of the ox-eye daisies, chicory and purple knapweed and vetch, and a vole pokes its head out of an old can which has been carelessly thrown away.

Further on, where the old track goes through a wood, ferns and mosses nestle in the damp coolness beneath the trees and a toad sits motionless on a stone. In places the ruts have filled with water and golden kingcups and rushes grow round them. The fallen trunk of a silver birch tree is

riddled with holes made by woodpeckers searching for insects, and clusters of bracket fungi are growing on the dead wood. A fox hurries away round the corner. He has to be careful when people are about.

Just beyond the wood the foxes have their earth under the hedgerow of sweet chestnut and dog-rose bushes. With only the cows looking on, the vixen rolls in the loose earth and the dog fox sniffs cautiously at a large toad which he has disturbed from its resting place. He knows it has a nasty taste and he'd better stick to eating rabbits, birds, rats and mice, if he can catch them. Though all is quiet here now, the foxes have to watch out for danger. A track like this is popular with people with guns.

A stream runs across the track further down and into the pond in the field beyond. The great willow tree likes the damp, so do the reedmace and the sedge growing in front of it at the edge of the water. It's very quiet today.

A fish jumps and startles the heron. The otters playing on the other side of the pond look up too. After some rain, young toads have come out to sit on the waterlily leaves, while the old toad tries in vain to catch a large dragonfly. In the reeds a pair of reed warblers are also looking for insects to eat. How safe is that damsel fly?

As the track winds up the hill again it runs close to more of the farm company's neat fields. But the edge by the old track is unkempt. It's overgrown with tall yellow golden rod, the pink spears of willowherb, clumps of mauve michaelmas daisies and, below them, poppies, ragwort and sunspurge. A flock of sparrows feeds on the seeds. The dog fox hunts along the far side of the field and some harvest mice have woven a nest among the barley stalks.

At the highest part of the track there is a fine view of the surrounding countryside with big new grain silos in the distance. Here the track passes round an outcrop of sandstone where butterflies sun their wings and banded snails cluster on nearby plants.

A thrush has been feeding, using a flat stone to smash open the shells of the snails it likes to eat. Judging by the owl pellets lying on the other stone, that tawny owl flying over the fields in the late afternoon rests here between meals. One of the pellets he coughed up has broken open. It is full of all the indigestible bits, like the fur and bones, of the mice and voles he fed on.

From round the corner where brambles, red campion and sweet cicely flank the track you can see down to the old farm at last. But far from being deserted today it seems to be a centre of activity.

At the bottom of the hill a surveyor stands with a special measuring instrument called a theodolite, ready to check the

rise of the land all the way up to another one at the top. He seems to have big changes in mind. It looks as if the peace of the old farm is about to be disturbed; already the swallows that nested in the ruined buildings are flying away, and the tawny owl's home in the dead tree may not last long either.

But what's going to happen?

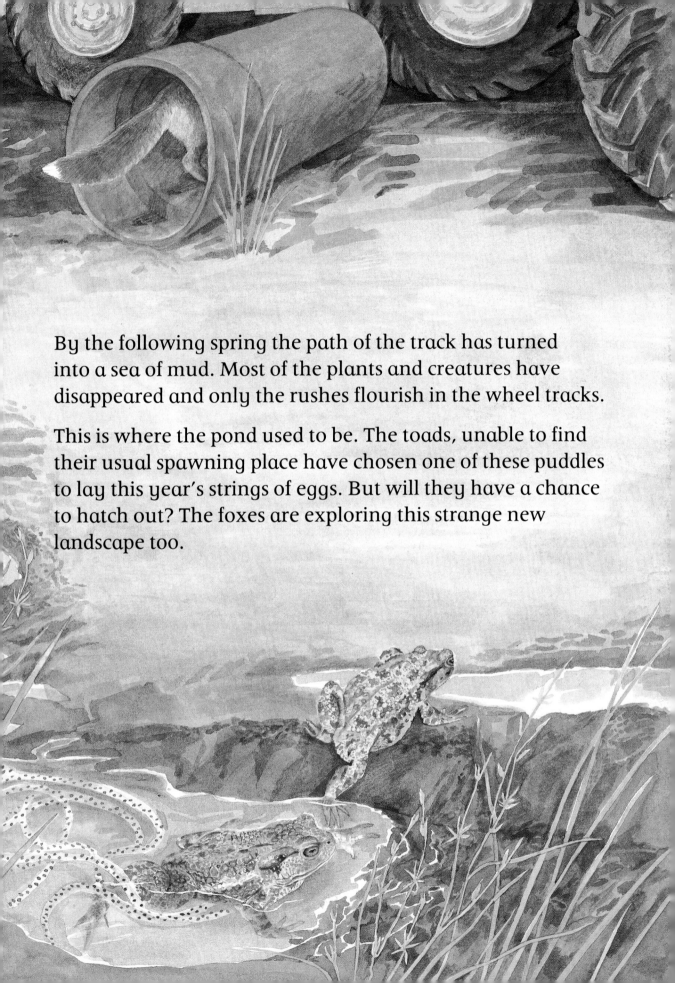

By the following spring the path of the track has turned into a sea of mud. Most of the plants and creatures have disappeared and only the rushes flourish in the wheel tracks.

This is where the pond used to be. The toads, unable to find their usual spawning place have chosen one of these puddles to lay this year's strings of eggs. But will they have a chance to hatch out? The foxes are exploring this strange new landscape too.

By the summer, despite the upheaval that continues all around, some plants and animals have made themselves at home. Today is a Sunday and all is quiet. Sparrows peck at the watchman's sandwiches when he goes into his hut, starlings perch boldly by the steps and one of the foxes even searches for titbits in the rubbish sacks. Although it's only been there a short time, the raw mound of earth is covered with new growth. Flowers like shepherd's purse, golden rod and the bright blue cornflowers, which grow quickly from seed in the disturbed soil, attract the butterflies, and the ragwort is covered with cinnabar moth caterpillars.

At last the work is finished. So this was what it was all for! Where the old track used to wind, a great, straight, six-lane road is ready for the traffic. Hedgerows have gone, but the wood is still there and the verges are seeded with grass and summer flowers that feed the butterflies again.

The kestrel now hunts for mice and voles at the side of the road, and at night maybe even the owl returns. Along the central reservation the ragwort and the cranesbill with its pointed seed capsules are flourishing. In between, ink cap fungus has sprung up after last night's rain.

It is spring again. Where the hill once used to rise above the old farmhouse, now the road runs through a deep cutting in the sandstone. The rocky walls on either side are already riddled with the nest holes of sand martins. One bird is busy enlarging the hole to make room for the baby birds which will soon hatch out.

Despite the cars roaring past only a few metres away, the vixen dozes peacefully in the sun. She knows that her cubs are safe to chase butterflies, so long as they don't stray on the road. People are not allowed to walk here any more and that means no guns. The stinging nettles don't bother the foxes either.

The road builders have done a good job. They have laid a pipe under the road to carry the stream to a big new pond on the other side. This also gives the toads a safe way through from their home in the woods to their mating grounds in the pond. The reed warblers may return to the pond soon, but sadly there is no sign of the otters, not even their footprints or their droppings, or of the heron. Perhaps there are no fish yet for them to eat.

Everything still looks a bit bare but reeds and water plants are beginning to grow at the edges and a pair of ducks are rearing their first batch of ducklings. The road doesn't seem to bother them, or the swallows, back again for another summer.

the new road

the new
pond